A Random House TELL ME ABOUT Book

RAINFOREST ANIMALS

By Michael Chinery

Illustrated by David Holmes
& Bernard Robinson

Random House 🏠 New York

First American edition, 1992.

Copyright © 1991 by Grisewood & Dempsey Ltd.
All rights reserved under International and Pan-American
Copyright Conventions. Published in the United States by
Random House, Inc., New York. Originally published in Great
Britain by Kingfisher Books, a Grisewood & Dempsey Company,
in 1991.

Library of Congress Cataloging in Publication Data
Chinery, Michael.
Rainforest animals / by Michael Chinery;
illustrated by David Holmes and Bernard Robinson.
p. cm. — (A Random House tell me about book)
Includes index.
Summary: Introduces animals of the rainforest and how they
live, including the howler monkey, toucan, and deadly arrow-
poison frog.
1. Rainforest fauna—Juvenile literature. [1. Rainforest
animals.] I. Holmes, David, ill. II. Robinson, Bernard, ill.
III. Title. IV. Series.
QL112.C55 1992 591.909′52—dc20 91-53143
ISBN 0-679-82047-7
ISBN 0-679-92047-1 (lib. bdg.)

Manufactured in Hong Kong
1   2   3   4   5   6   7   8   9   10

Contents

Life in the rainforests

Rainforests grow in places where there is lots of rain. Most rainforests are found in the tropics, on either side of the equator. Most of the plants there are evergreen — they never drop their leaves, but grow all year round in the hot, steamy atmosphere. Animals live at all levels in the forest, from the ground to the treetops.

RAINFOREST FACTS

● About 125 acres of tropical rainforest are cut down every minute — that's an area of almost 100 football fields.

● The tallest trees in the tropical rainforest are 165 feet high.

DO YOU KNOW

Some rainforests are huge, but altogether they still cover only about one-twentieth of the earth's surface. Even so, scientists believe that the rainforests contain more than half of the world's plant and animal species.

TROPICAL RAINFORESTS

Tropical rainforests are found around the world in areas near the equator. For this reason they are sometimes called equatorial rainforests. The three main tropical rainforest regions are around the Amazon River in South America, in central Africa, and in Indonesia. Over half of the world's rainforests are found in South America.

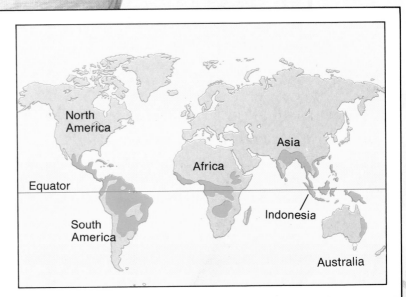

Gorillas – gentle giants of the forest

Gorillas are the largest of the apes. People once thought they were fierce and dangerous, but they are actually gentle and friendly creatures. They roam the African rainforest in small groups and feed almost entirely on leaves. Each group is ruled by an old male. He decides where the group will feed each day.

GORILLA FACTS

- Large male gorillas are nearly 6 feet tall and weigh 450 pounds.

- Gorillas may live for up to 35 years.

The group leader is always an old male with silvery hair on his back. He is called a silverback.

Gorillas have superb eyesight, and the leader keeps a watchful eye on the whole group.

Male gorillas thump their chests when they are angry, or just to show off their great strength.

Gorillas like to sit together in the middle of the day. Females spend a lot of time grooming their babies.

SURVIVAL WATCH

Gorillas are big animals and have nothing to fear from other wild animals. People are their main problem. We keep cutting down the forests, and if this continues, the gorillas will have nowhere to live. The World Wide Fund for Nature and other organizations are working hard to save the gorillas. They are raising money to create special reserves where the animals can live in safety.

DO YOU KNOW

Gorillas make cozy beds every night with leafy branches. Females often sleep in the trees, but big males have to make their beds down on the ground.

7

The lemurs of Madagascar

Lemurs are distant cousins of monkeys. There are 22 different kinds, and they live only on the African island of Madagascar. They have survived there for millions of years because there have never been any monkeys on the island to compete with them. Most lemurs roam the forests in small groups. Some are active at night, but most of them feed in the daytime. They eat fruit, leaves, bark, and insects.

Ring-tailed lemurs are the only lemurs that spend much time on the ground. They live in groups of up to 30 animals.

THE BOUNCING INDRI

The indri is the biggest lemur. It is over 2 feet long, but its tail is tiny. It makes spectacular leaps through the trees. On the ground it bounces along on its big back legs.

SURVIVAL WATCH

Lemurs are much less common than they were 100 years ago. Some are in real danger of extinction because the forests of Madagascar are being destroyed. But recently people have realized that the lemurs are great tourist attractions, and special reserves are being set up for them.

The tail of the ring-tailed lemur is up to 2 feet long and is used to signal to other groups of lemurs that the area is occupied.

THE NOCTURNAL AYE-AYE

The cat-sized aye-aye is a strange and rare lemur. Its big eyes and ears show that it is a nocturnal creature — it comes out at night. It scoops out insects from tree trunks with its hook-like middle finger. The aye-aye also uses this slender finger to comb its fur. During the day the aye-aye spends its time in a hollow tree or among branches.

The devil's flower – a tricky insect

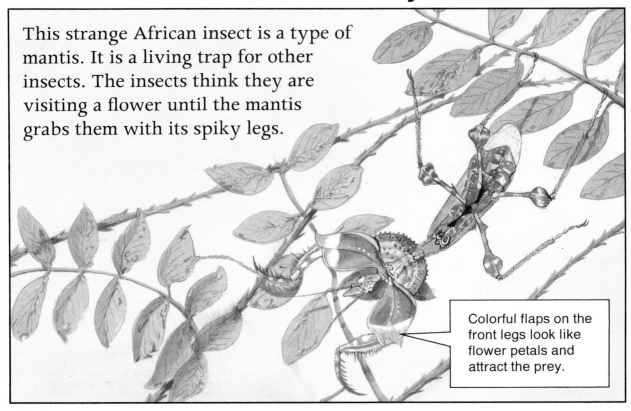

This strange African insect is a type of mantis. It is a living trap for other insects. The insects think they are visiting a flower until the mantis grabs them with its spiky legs.

Colorful flaps on the front legs look like flower petals and attract the prey.

The colorful mandrill

Mandrills are ground-living monkeys from the forests of central Africa. The red on the male's face gets brighter if he becomes angry.

MANDRILL FACTS

• Mandrills live in family groups and talk to each other with grunts. They sleep in the trees.

• Females and young are not as brightly colored as the males.

A mandrill walks on its hands and feet. Its long fingers are useful for gathering food and carrying it to its mouth.

The chubby colobus monkey

Colobus monkeys live in Africa and feed only on leaves. They have to eat lots of leaves to get enough nourishment, so they have big stomachs and always look fat. They sit around more than other monkeys because they need more time to digest their food.

The colobus has no thumbs. Its hands simply hook over the branches as it swings through the trees.

The tail cannot curl around branches like the tails of American monkeys (page 18).

The big-eyed tarsier

Tarsiers are little relatives of monkeys. They feed on all sorts of small animals, which they find with their sharp eyes and ears. They leap onto their prey and kill it with their teeth.

 SURVIVAL WATCH

Tarsiers live in the forests of Southeast Asia. They are quite common in some places, but their numbers are falling fast as the forests are being destroyed.

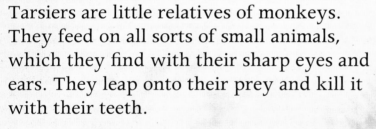

Big eyes enable the tarsier to see well at night. Big ears also give the animal excellent hearing.

Chimpanzees – our nearest relatives

Chimpanzees are apes. They are our closest relatives among the wild animals. They live in the forests of Africa and feed mainly on fruit. Chimps were once thought to feed entirely on plants, but they eat quite a lot of meat as well. They often kill pigs and antelope. Male chimps sometimes work in teams to trap monkeys in the trees. If they find plenty of food, the males make drumming noises on the tree trunks to call other chimps to the feast.

Some chimps have learned to use sticks to crack nuts and get at the juicy kernels inside them.

Chimps often throw sticks and stones at their enemies.

Chimps like to catch and eat tasty termites by poking sticks into their nests.

The expression on this chimp's face as it grooms one of its babies shows that it is concentrating hard on the task.

Chimps make simple beds for themselves by weaving thin, leafy branches together. They do not make new beds every night.

CHIMP FACTS

• Chimps live in groups of up to 100 animals. The group leader is usually the noisiest male. Males often quarrel with each other, but female chimps are usually all good friends.

• Male chimps weigh up to 110 pounds and are about 5 feet high when they stand up. Female chimps are a bit smaller.

The fearsome crowned eagle

The crowned eagle is the most powerful bird in the African forest. It catches monkeys in the trees and even snatches small antelope from the forest floor. Large wings give it the power to carry animals heavier than itself.

Crowned eagles have to be fast to catch monkeys in the trees. They kill their prey with their huge talons.

? DO YOU KNOW

The crowned eagle weighs about 9 pounds and is about 2½ feet long. It gets its name from the big crest of feathers on its head. Village chiefs once used the feathers in their headdresses.

The talented tailorbird

The tailorbird makes its nest by sewing leaves together to form a pouch. Using its long beak as a needle, it sews with thin fibers pulled from plants and with silk from spiders' webs.

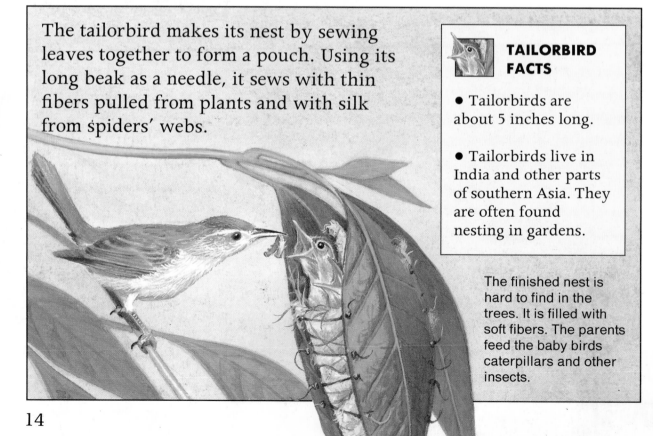

TAILORBIRD FACTS

● Tailorbirds are about 5 inches long.

● Tailorbirds live in India and other parts of southern Asia. They are often found nesting in gardens.

The finished nest is hard to find in the trees. It is filled with soft fibers. The parents feed the baby birds caterpillars and other insects.

Hard-headed hornbills

Hornbills live in Africa and Asia. These birds have enormous beaks that help them reach fruit growing far out on slender twigs. Hornbills nest in tree holes. When a female has settled into a suitable hole, she blocks the entrance with mud brought by the male. She leaves just enough room to push her beak out and stays locked up until her eggs hatch. Her mate brings food to her several times a day.

There are 45 different kinds of hornbill. They vary in size from 1½ feet to over 4 feet. This one is a Great Indian hornbill.

Army ants on the move

Africa's army ants hunt in long columns. They swarm over any animal in their path and tear it to pieces with their jaws. They have no permanent homes. When they have eaten everything around them they march off to camp in another area of the forest.

Millions of small worker ants march in the column. Each one will carry bits of food back to the camp.

Large soldier ants march beside the column and defend it with their great jaws.

? DO YOU KNOW

Some Africans use the soldier ants to mend wounds. They make the ants bite into the skin on each side of a cut and then snip off the ants' heads. The jaws stay closed and hold the skin together until the wound heals.

Clever weaver ants

Weaver ants make baglike nests with living leaves. One group of ants holds the leaves in place with their jaws and feet while other ants run between them with grubs, or baby ants, in their jaws. The grubs produce sticky silk threads that glue the leaves together.

Weaver ants live in trees and bushes and eat other insects. They kill the insects with their large jaws or by spraying them with poison.

Leaf-cutter ants

South America's leaf-cutter ants are the farmers of the ant world. They grow all their own food. Worker ants climb the forest trees and cut small pieces from the leaves. They carry the pieces back to their underground nests, where other workers cut them into smaller pieces and spread them out in special "gardens." The leaves soon get moldy, and the ants harvest the mold and eat it. They even fertilize the gardens with their own droppings to make sure they get good crops.

 DO YOU KNOW

Leaf-cutters are also called parasol ants because they carry leaves home over their heads like parasols, or sunshades.

Leaf-cutter ants have big-toothed jaws to slice through the leaves like scissors.

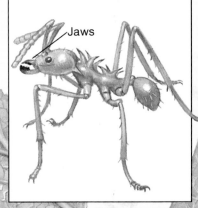
Jaws

Worker ants bring thousands of leaf fragments back to the nest every night, holding them firmly in their jaws.

The workers may travel over 300 feet to cut their leaves. Larger ants called soldiers guard the workers' route.

 LEAF-CUTTER FACTS

• Leaf-cutter ants live on farms and in gardens as well as in forests. They destroy all kinds of crops, usually stripping every leaf from a plant before moving on.

The noisy howler monkey

Howler monkeys are among the noisiest animals in the forest. They live in groups, and every morning when they wake up, they start to howl and bark. These noisy choruses tell other groups of howlers that the area is occupied and warn them to keep away. The monkeys can then feed in peace. They howl again as they settle down for the night.

Howler monkeys live in groups of up to 30 animals. They stay close together as they search for food in the treetops.

? DO YOU KNOW

Like most other South American monkeys, the howler can wrap its tail around branches and use it like an extra arm or leg as it swings through the trees. African and Asian monkeys cannot do this.

The howler's loud voice comes from its large throat pouch. Males have bigger pouches and louder voices than females.

HOWLER FACTS

• The howler's voice can carry for about $1\frac{1}{2}$ miles through the forest.

• Howler monkeys are black or brownish red.

• Their favorite food is wild figs.

Color-changing chameleons

Chameleons are slow-moving lizards that live in the trees. Many different kinds live in the forests of Africa. Although a chameleon moves slowly, it is very skilled at catching insects. It traps them with its long, sticky tongue which it shoots out at high speed. The chameleon has an excellent aim and rarely misses its target.

The chameleon has a flexible tail and can wrap it around twigs for extra support and safety.

Chameleon eyes can turn in any direction. The animal can even look forward with one eye and backward with the other.

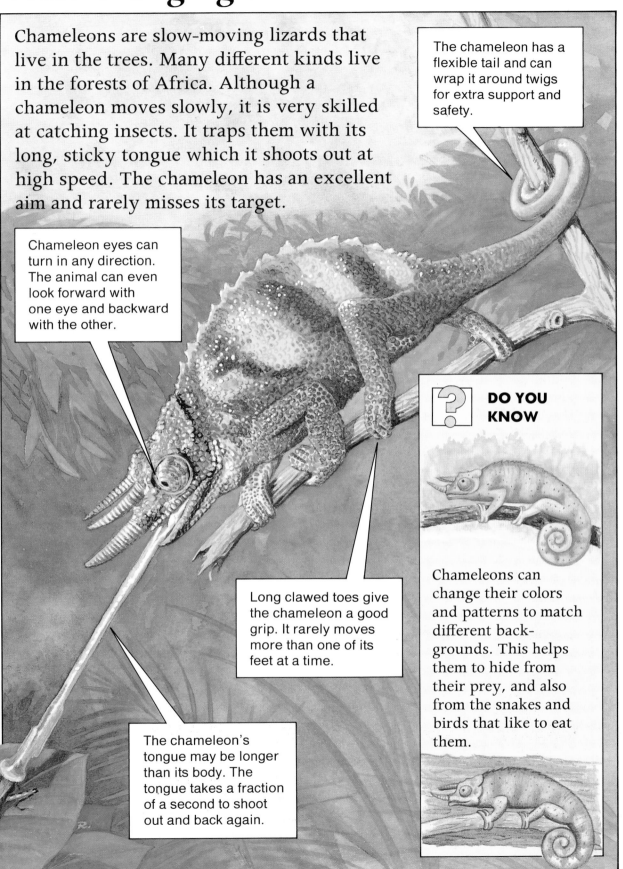

? DO YOU KNOW

Chameleons can change their colors and patterns to match different backgrounds. This helps them to hide from their prey, and also from the snakes and birds that like to eat them.

Long clawed toes give the chameleon a good grip. It rarely moves more than one of its feet at a time.

The chameleon's tongue may be longer than its body. The tongue takes a fraction of a second to shoot out and back again.

The athletic leopard

The leopard is a powerful cat that lives in many parts of Africa and southern Asia. It likes open, rocky country as well as forests, and it is a wonderful climber of both rocks and trees. Leopards usually live alone and feed both day and night. Their prey includes pigs, antelope, monkeys, and dogs. A favorite trick is to lie on a branch and drop onto passing prey.

A leopard often uses its great strength to drag the bodies of its victims high into trees, where the meat will be safe from hyenas and other scavengers.

Its spotted coat makes the leopard hard to see in the patchwork of light and shade among the forest trees.

 DO YOU KNOW

No two leopards have exactly the same coat pattern. In the wettest areas, a leopard's fur is often completely black. These black leopards are commonly known as panthers.

The jaguar – America's leopard

The jaguar is the leopard's powerful American cousin. It lives mainly in the dense forests of South and Central America, usually close to water. It is an excellent swimmer and climber. Jaguars feed mainly on wild pigs and large rodents. They also sprawl by the water and scoop up fish with their huge paws. They even catch alligators and turtles.

Like the leopard, the jaguar is well camouflaged when stalking through the light and shade of the forest.

Jaguar spots form rings like those of the leopard, but a jaguar's rings are different — nearly all of them have a spot in the middle.

SURVIVAL WATCH

Jaguars and other spotted cats have long been hunted for their fur. Many jaguars have also been killed because they attack farm animals such as sheep. Jaguars have disappeared from many farming areas, but they are not yet in danger of total extinction, as they are found over a huge area — from Mexico to Chile and Argentina.

JAGUAR FACTS

● Jaguars are about as long as leopards, but much heavier. They weigh up to 300 pounds.

● A female jaguar has up to four cubs at a time. They stay with her for two years.

Playful toucans

Toucans have some of the world's biggest beaks. The beak is sometimes longer than the rest of the body. These birds live in small flocks and use their colorful beaks like flags to signal one another. Toucans also make loud drumming noises by hitting branches with their beaks. They even have friendly "pillow fights," in which they whack each other with their beaks until one bird falls off the branch.

DO YOU KNOW

Toucans live in South and Central America. They look similar to the hornbills of Africa and Asia (page 15), but the two families of birds are not related. They look alike because they live in a similar way, hopping from branch to branch to gather food.

Hornbill

Toucans feed mainly on fruit. They also eat frogs and insects, and sometimes steal eggs and chicks from the nests of other birds.

TOUCAN FACTS

- There are about 40 kinds of toucans.

- Males have longer beaks than females.

- Toucans nest in holes in trees.

The large beak is really very light. Inside it is mostly air, with a mesh of tiny bones supporting the outer shell.

Macaws – living nutcrackers

Macaws are the world's largest parrots. There are several different kinds, and they all live in South America. The macaw is one of the world's best nutcrackers. Its hooked beak can open a Brazil nut with ease — and it can cut off a finger just as easily! The bird first uses the edge of its beak like a saw to cut partway through the shell. Opening the nut is then simple. The macaw also uses its beak as an extra foot when climbing.

The top and bottom parts of the macaw's beak rub against each other and keep the edges sharp.

Two of the toes face forward and two face backward. This makes it easy for the macaw to pick things up and grip them.

SURVIVAL WATCH

Macaws are becoming rare because their forest home is being destroyed. They are also caught and sold as pets. Macaws are very good at imitating humans and can learn lots of words, but they don't know what the words mean. Some South American Indians use macaw feathers for decoration.

The ocelot

The ocelot is a cat about 4 feet long, including its tail. It lives in the forests of South and Central America and southwestern North America, and is a superb climber.

SURVIVAL WATCH

Thousands of ocelots used to be killed every year to make fur coats. Selling the skins is now against the law, but the ocelot is still in danger from the destruction of the forests.

The dangling kinkajou

The kinkajou looks like a monkey, especially when hanging from its long tail. It lives in the forests of Central and South America. It is a good climber, but does not leap from tree to tree like a monkey.

KINKAJOU FACTS

● The kinkajou's body is about 8 inches long, and its tail adds another 18 inches.

● It is more closely related to bears than to monkeys.

The topsy-turvy sloth

The sloth does nearly everything upside down. It spends almost all its life hanging upside down in the trees of South and Central America. One of the slowest of all mammals, it may spend its whole life in a single tree. It feeds on leaves and fruits. When a sloth comes down to the ground, it cannot walk, but drags itself along with its long claws.

SLOTH FACTS

● Sloths are between $1\frac{1}{2}$ and 3 feet long.

● Their top speed through the branches is half a mile per hour. It is even less on the ground!

Sloths hang from huge hook-like claws. There are several kinds of sloths, some with only two claws on the front feet.

Tiny plants called algae grow in the sloth's fur and make it green. Caterpillars also live there and feed on the algae.

The sloth has one baby at a time. The baby clings tightly to its mother for several weeks.

The fur of mammals usually runs from the back to the belly. Sloth fur lies in the other direction so that rain runs off easily.

Hummingbirds – jewels of the forest

Hummingbirds are brilliantly colored birds named for the humming noise they make with their rapidly beating wings. They dart quickly from place to place and can even hover and fly backward. There are over 300 species, all living in North, Central, and South America. Hummingbirds feed on nectar and insects. They use up so much energy in flight that they have to eat more than their own weight in food every day.

THE SWORDBILL

The swordbill hummingbird's body is only about 3 inches long, but its sword-like beak is up to 5 inches long. The swordbill can also poke its slender tongue out another 1 or 2 inches. With this amazing equipment, the bird can get nectar from deep bell-shaped or tubular flowers.

When a hummingbird is hovering, its wings whir like tiny propellers, beating up to 75 times every second. This is what produces the humming noise.

Hummingbirds suck sugary nectar from flowers while they are hovering. They also catch small insects and spiders.

Hummingbirds make their nests with spider silk and pieces of bark or lichen. Hovering parents feed their chicks by pumping nectar and insects into their gaping beaks.

HUMMINGBIRD FACTS

● The biggest species of hummingbird is only 8 inches long.

● The smallest type is the bee hummingbird of Cuba. It is under $2\frac{1}{2}$ inches long, including its beak and tail. It is the smallest of all birds.

● Some hummingbirds can fly 60 mph (miles per hour) over short distances.

The majestic tiger

The tiger is the largest member of the cat family. It lives in the forests of Asia, and also by rivers where there is plenty of tall grass in which it can hide. The tiger is not a fast runner and, like most cats, it silently stalks its prey. When it is close enough, it leaps out and knocks its prey down with one swipe of a great paw. Deer, pigs, and antelope are the tiger's main prey. It usually hunts alone and at night.

The tiger uses its large dagger-like teeth to stab its prey. One bite in the throat or the back of the neck is enough to kill a deer.

 SURVIVAL WATCH

Many tigers have been shot for their beautiful fur or because they have killed farm animals. Much of the tiger's forest home has been destroyed to make way for farms, so the animal is now in real danger. There may be only a few hundred tigers left.

 DO YOU KNOW

Tigers don't enjoy the heat. They spend really hot days lying in pools and streams.

The tiger's roar can be heard over 1 mile away. It roars to defend its territory and to call its mate and cubs.

The tiger's striped coat camouflages it well as it stalks through the grass. Its unsuspecting prey is taken completely by surprise.

The flying fox

The flying fox is not a fox at all. It is a large fruit-eating bat with a face like a fox. Several kinds live in tropical Asia and Australia. They live in big flocks, eating valuable fruit crops and damaging trees.

The bat's wing is made of flexible skin stretched over long fingers. The wings span nearly 5 feet, but the bat weighs only 2 pounds.

The tree frog

Tree frogs live high in the forest trees of Southeast Asia. Flaps of skin between their toes act like parachutes, helping the frogs to glide gently from one tree to the next as they search for insects to eat.

Some tree frogs lay their eggs in the trees. They lay them in packets of foam wrapped in leaves. When the eggs hatch, the tiny tadpoles drop down to live in pools on the ground.

Sticky pads on the tree frog's toes help it to climb. Using these pads, it can cling to even the smoothest of leaves.

The agile orangutan

Orangutans live only on the islands of Borneo and Sumatra in Southeast Asia. Their name, meaning "man of the woods," is appropriate because an orangutan's face looks much like a human face. Orangutans spend most of their time in the trees, and although they are slower than gibbons (see facing page), they are amazing climbers.

The orang's legs are not as strong as its arms, but its long toes help it grip the branches as it climbs.

Like other apes, the orang has no tail. It has long red hair, but it is not as hairy all over as most apes.

SURVIVAL WATCH

The orangutan is very rare because its forest home is being rapidly destroyed. Orangs are also caught and sold as pets. Special reserves have been set up so that the remaining few animals can live in safety.

The acrobatic gibbon

Gibbons are built for life high in the trees. They move through the treetops at high speed, usually by swinging hand over hand along the branches. Their powerful arms are actually longer than their legs. Gibbons live in family groups and make a lot of noise to let other groups know where they are. They feed mainly on fruit.

Gibbons often leap from tree to tree. Long, strong fingers give them a secure grip on the branches.

GIBBON FACTS

● There are several different kinds of gibbons, and they all live in Southeast Asia.

● Gibbons look like monkeys, but they have no tails and they are really small apes.

Gibbons have no nests, so the baby has to go wherever its mother goes. It clings tightly to her as she swings through the branches.

The gibbon has a wonderful sense of balance. It uses its arms to steady itself as it walks along thin branches.

The proud peacock

The peacock has some of the world's biggest feathers. He spreads them into a magnificent fan when he sees a female. If she likes the display, she will become his mate. Peacocks eat almost anything, from seeds to mice and snakes. Although they eat on the ground, they sleep in the trees at night. They often live around villages.

PEACOCK FACTS

- Peacocks live in India and Sri Lanka.

- Males are over 8 feet long, including the train of feathers.

- Peacocks are very noisy birds, with piercing screams.

While displaying, the peacock shakes his feathers from time to time and produces a loud rattling noise.

Some of the feathers are over 3 feet long. When he is not displaying, the bird folds his fan up and drags it behind him.

The female is called a peahen. She is less colorful than the male. She lays up to 20 eggs in a nest on the ground.

Show-off birds of paradise

Birds of paradise have some of the most beautiful feathers in the world. To attract females, the males dance and show off their long, colorful plumes. They perform many of their dances while hanging upside down like trapeze artists. Birds of paradise live in the forests of New Guinea and northern Australia. The one shown here is the red-plumed bird of paradise.

2. He then flutters his wings and bends forward. At the end of his dance he is hanging upside down from the branch.

1. The male begins his courtship dance by lifting his wings and spreading out his beautiful red plumes.

SURVIVAL WATCH

Birds of paradise used to be killed so their feathers could be used on women's hats. Today the feathers are used for headdresses.

The females are dull in color. They choose their mates after watching the males' displays.

Beautiful birdwing butterflies

Birdwings get their name because they seem more like birds than butterflies when they fly overhead. They live in the forests of Southeast Asia, New Guinea, and northern Australia and include some of the world's biggest and most beautiful butterflies. Many species have become rare because butterfly collectors have caught so many. The destruction of their forest homes is making them even rarer.

This is Rajah Brooke's birdwing, from Malaysia and Indonesia. Thousands are caught every year, but this species is still quite common in some areas.

DO YOU KNOW

Female birdwings usually stay high in the trees. Many of them are dull brown, but female Rajah Brooke's birdwings are nearly as bright as the males.

BIRDWING FACTS

● The largest species is Queen Alexandra's birdwing, with wings over 10 inches across.

● The wings of many species are used to make jewelry.

The wing colors often change as you look at the butterfly from different angles.

Deadly arrow-poison frogs

Arrow-poison frogs are the most poisonous animals on earth. They carry deadly poison in their skin. The South American Choco Indians use this poison on the tips of their hunting arrows. A tiny scratch from a poisoned arrow can kill a large animal such as a jaguar. Animals killed by the arrows are safe to eat because the poison is destroyed when it is swallowed.

 DO YOU KNOW

The male carries the eggs and tadpoles on his back. The tadpoles feed on food stored in the eggs. When the food has gone, the male sets the tadpoles free in water.

POISON FROG FACTS

● Some arrow-poison frogs are so poisonous that one gram of poison is enough to kill 100,000 people.

● Some species are under 1 inch long.

Arrow-poison frogs have brilliant colors, warning other rain-forest animals that they are poisonous and should be left alone.

Most arrow-poison frogs have suction pads on their toes, helping them to cling safely to wet and shiny leaves.

The Indian elephant – lord of the forest

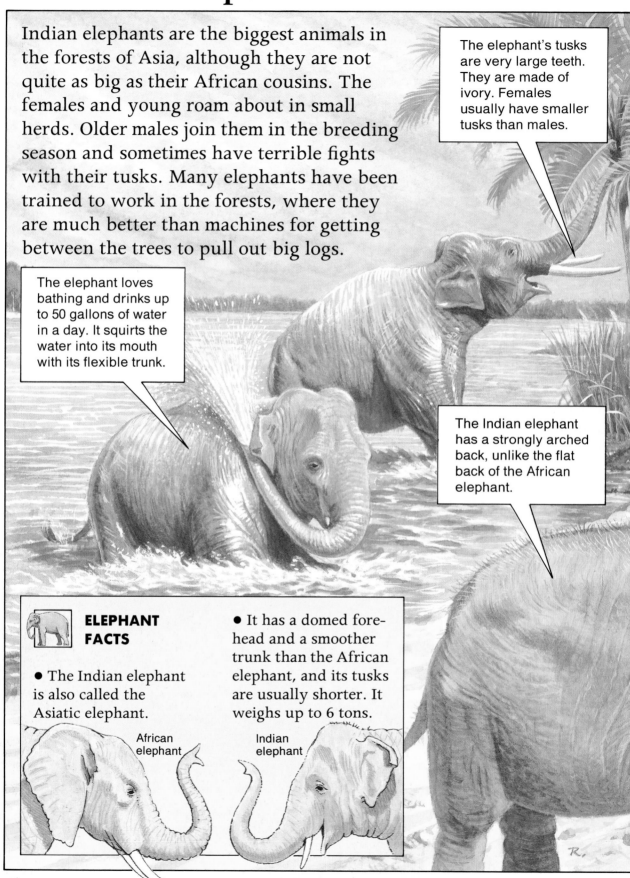

Indian elephants are the biggest animals in the forests of Asia, although they are not quite as big as their African cousins. The females and young roam about in small herds. Older males join them in the breeding season and sometimes have terrible fights with their tusks. Many elephants have been trained to work in the forests, where they are much better than machines for getting between the trees to pull out big logs.

The elephant's tusks are very large teeth. They are made of ivory. Females usually have smaller tusks than males.

The elephant loves bathing and drinks up to 50 gallons of water in a day. It squirts the water into its mouth with its flexible trunk.

The Indian elephant has a strongly arched back, unlike the flat back of the African elephant.

ELEPHANT FACTS

● The Indian elephant is also called the Asiatic elephant.

● It has a domed forehead and a smoother trunk than the African elephant, and its tusks are usually shorter. It weighs up to 6 tons.

African elephant

Indian elephant

An elephant can drag huge logs from the forest and pick them up with its trunk and tusks. Each elephant has its own rider.

Indian elephants are not in as much danger as African elephants, but they are much less common than they were 100 years ago. The forests in which they live are gradually being destroyed, and the odd thing about this is that tamed working elephants are helping to cause the damage. Large areas of forest must be pre-served in order to protect Asia's wild elephants.

Elephants feed almost entirely on leaves, which they pull from the trees and shove into their mouths with their trunks.

The ears do not reach down as far as the mouth. They are much smaller than the ears of an African elephant.

Rainforests in danger

Rainforests are among the most threatened places on earth. Millions of trees are cut down each year for timber. Huge areas are cleared every day to make way for farming. Thousands of animals are probably becoming extinct every year because there is nowhere left for them to live. Even if new trees are planted, these places will never get their original wildlife back again.

Many kinds of beautiful forest birds and insects will never be seen again because their forest homes are being cut down. The problem is especially bad in South America and Southeast Asia.

GREENHOUSE EFFECT

Every time we breathe, we give off a gas called carbon dioxide. The same gas is made by car engines and whenever something is burned. It forms a layer around the earth and traps heat, just like greenhouse glass. The heat warms the earth and can cause droughts and other big changes in the world's weather. Trees use up carbon dioxide, so cutting down the rainforests is making this "greenhouse effect" even worse.

Useful words

Algae   A group of simple plants that usually live in water and damp places. Many of them are very small.

Ape   Any of the large monkey-like animals that are our own closest relatives in the animal world. Gorillas, chimpanzees, orangutans, and gibbons are all apes. They differ from monkeys in that they have no tails.

Camouflage   The way in which animals avoid the attention of their enemies by resembling or blending in with their surroundings.

Courtship   The process of attracting a mate. Animals often do this by showing off their bright colors.

Equator   The imaginary line running around the center of the earth. This divides the earth into two halves called the Northern and Southern Hemispheres.

Evergreen   A tree or shrub that keeps its leaves throughout the year.

Extinct   An animal is extinct when it no longer exists anywhere in the world. Many types of animals are in danger of becoming extinct.

Hover   To remain at one place in the air, without moving forward or backward. Hummingbirds hover by beating their wings very rapidly.

Mammal   Any animal that feeds its babies with milk from the mother's body. Mammals live almost everywhere, and there are many types in the rainforests, including monkeys, leopards, and elephants.

Nature reserve   An area set aside to protect wild plants and animals — often rare ones that are in danger of becoming extinct.

Nectar   The sugary juice produced by flowers. Many insects and birds feed on it.

Nocturnal   Active during the night.

Predator   Any animal that hunts or traps other animals for food. Predators can also be the prey of other animals.

Prey   An animal that is caught and eaten by a predator.

Scavenger   An animal that feeds mainly on dead matter — especially one that clears up the remains of another animal's meal.

Species   A species is any one particular kind of animal or plant, such as a tiger or a mahogany tree.

Tadpole   The early stage in the life of a frog or a toad after hatching from an egg.

Termite   Termites are small insects that live in large colonies — often in tree trunks or in mounds of soil. They are common in most tropical areas and are eaten by all kinds of other creatures.

Territory   The area in which an animal or group of animals lives. Animals defend their territory against other animals of the same kind.

Tropical   Having to do with the tropics. These are warm areas of the world, on either side of the equator.

Index